Personal I

MW00816572

Name:

Address:

City: State: Zip:

Phone:

Fax: Cell/Pager:

Email:

Emergency Phone Numbers

Police: Pediatrician:

Fire Station: Dentist:

Poison Control: Service Garage:

Doctor: Towing:

School Phone Numbers

2016

JANUARY

S	M	T	W	T	F	S
					1	2
3	4	5	6	7	8	9
10	11	12	13	14	15	16
17	18	19	20	21	22	23
24/31	25	26	27	28	29	30

FEBRUARY

S	M	T	W	T	F	S
	1	2	3	4	5	6
7	8	9	10	11	12	13
14	15	16	17	18	19	20
21	22	23	24	25	26	27
28	29					

MARCH

S	M	T	W	T	F	S
		1	2	3	4	5
6	7	8	9	10	11	12
13	14	15	16	17	18	19
20	21	22	23	24	25	26
27	28	29	30	31		

APRIL

S	M	T	W	T	F	S
					1	2
3	4	5	6	7	8	9
10	11	12	13	14	15	16
17	18	19	20	21	22	23
24	25	26	27	28	29	30

MAY

S	M	T	W	T	F	S
1	2	3	4	5	6	7
8	9	10	11	12	13	14
15	16	17	18	19	20	21
22	23	24	25	26	27	28
29	30	31				

JUNE

S	M	T	W	T	F	S
			1	2	3	4
5	6	7	8	9	10	11
12	13	14	15	16	17	18
19	20	21	22	23	24	25
26	27	28	29	30		

JULY

S	M	T	W	T	F	S
					1	2
3	4	5	6	7	8	9
10	11	12	13	14	15	16
17	18	19	20	21	22	23
24/31	25	26	27	28	29	30

AUGUST

S	M	T	W	T	F	S
	1	2	3	4	5	6
7	8	9	10	11	12	13
14	15	16	17	18	19	20
21	22	23	24	25	26	27
28	29	30	31			

SEPTEMBER

S	M	T	W	T	F	S
				1	2	3
4	5	6	7	8	9	10
11	12	13	14	15	16	17
18	19	20	21	22	23	24
25	26	27	28	29	30	

OCTOBER

S	M	T	W	T	F	S
						1
2	3	4	5	6	7	8
9	10	11	12	13	14	15
16	17	18	19	20	21	22
23/30	24/31	25	26	27	28	29

NOVEMBER

S	M	T	W	T	F	S
		1	2	3	4	5
6	7	8	9	10	11	12
13	14	15	16	17	18	19
20	21	22	23	24	25	26
27	28	29	30			

DECEMBER

S	M	T	W	T	F	S
				1	2	3
4	5	6	7	8	9	10
11	12	13	14	15	16	17
18	19	20	21	22	23	24
25	26	27	28	29	30	31

2017

JANUARY

S	M	T	W	T	F	S
1	2	3	4	5	6	7
8	9	10	11	12	13	14
15	16	17	18	19	20	21
22	23	24	25	26	27	28
29	30	31				

FEBRUARY

S	M	T	W	T	F	S
			1	2	3	4
5	6	7	8	9	10	11
12	13	14	15	16	17	18
19	20	21	22	23	24	25
26	27	28				

MARCH

S	M	T	W	T	F	S
			1	2	3	4
5	6	7	8	9	10	11
12	13	14	15	16	17	18
19	20	21	22	23	24	25
26	27	28	29	30	31	

APRIL

S	M	T	W	T	F	S
						1
2	3	4	5	6	7	8
9	10	11	12	13	14	15
16	17	18	19	20	21	22
23/30	24	25	26	27	28	29

MAY

S	M	T	W	T	F	S
	1	2	3	4	5	6
7	8	9	10	11	12	13
14	15	16	17	18	19	20
21	22	23	24	25	26	27
28	29	30	31			

JUNE

S	M	T	W	T	F	S
				1	2	3
4	5	6	7	8	9	10
11	12	13	14	15	16	17
18	19	20	21	22	23	24
25	26	27	28	29	30	

JULY

S	M	T	W	T	F	S
						1
2	3	4	5	6	7	8
9	10	11	12	13	14	15
16	17	18	19	20	21	22
23/30	24/31	25	26	27	28	29

AUGUST

S	M	T	W	T	F	S
		1	2	3	4	5
6	7	8	9	10	11	12
13	14	15	16	17	18	19
20	21	22	23	24	25	26
27	28	29	30	31		

SEPTEMBER

S	M	T	W	T	F	S
					1	2
3	4	5	6	7	8	9
10	11	12	13	14	15	16
17	18	19	20	21	22	23
24	25	26	27	28	29	30

OCTOBER

S	M	T	W	T	F	S
1	2	3	4	5	6	7
8	9	10	11	12	13	14
15	16	17	18	19	20	21
22	23	24	25	26	27	28
29	30	31				

NOVEMBER

S	M	T	W	T	F	S
			1	2	3	4
5	6	7	8	9	10	11
12	13	14	15	16	17	18
19	20	21	22	23	24	25
26	27	28	29	30		

DECEMBER

S	M	T	W	T	F	S
					1	2
3	4	5	6	7	8	9
10	11	12	13	14	15	16
17	18	19	20	21	22	23
24/31	25	26	27	28	29	30

August

SUNDAY	MONDAY	TUESDAY	WEDNESDAY
July 2015 S M T W T F S 1 2 3 4 5 6 7 8 9 10 11 12 13 14 15 16 17 18 19 20 21 22 23 24 25 26 27 28 29 30 31	September 2015 S M T W T F S 1 2 3 4 5 6 7 8 9 10 11 12 13 14 15 16 17 18 19 20 21 22 23 24 25 26 27 28 29 30		
2	3 *Civic Holiday (CAN)*	4	5
9	10	11	12
16	17	18	19
23 / 30	24 / 31	25	26

2015

THURSDAY	FRIDAY	SATURDAY
		1
6	7	8
13	14	15
20	21	22
27	28	29

Monthly Projects

Grocery

Life isn't about getting and having, it's about giving and being.

—Kevin Kruse

To Do

July 2015

S	M	T	W	T	F	S
			1	2	3	4
5	6	7	8	9	10	11
12	13	14	15	16	17	18
19	20	21	22	23	24	25
26	27	28	29	30	31	

September 2015

S	M	T	W	T	F	S
		1	2	3	4	5
6	7	8	9	10	11	12
13	14	15	16	17	18	19
20	21	22	23	24	25	26
27	28	29	30			

2015 July/August

MONDAY
27

TUESDAY
28

WEDNESDAY
29

THURSDAY
30

FRIDAY *Full Moon*
31

SATURDAY
1

SUNDAY
2

Menus

Grocery

Whatever the mind of man can conceive and believe, it can achieve.

—Napoleon Hill

To Do

July 2015

S	M	T	W	T	F	S
			1	2	3	4
5	6	7	8	9	10	11
12	13	14	15	16	17	18
19	20	21	22	23	24	25
26	27	28	29	30	31	

September 2015

S	M	T	W	T	F	S
		1	2	3	4	5
6	7	8	9	10	11	12
13	14	15	16	17	18	19
20	21	22	23	24	25	26
27	28	29	30			

2015 August

MONDAY *Civic Holiday (CAN)*
3

TUESDAY
4

WEDNESDAY
5

THURSDAY
6

FRIDAY *Last Quarter Moon*
7

SATURDAY
8

SUNDAY
9

Menus

Grocery

Strive not to be a success, but rather to be of value.

—Albert Einstein

To Do

July 2015

S	M	T	W	T	F	S
			1	2	3	4
5	6	7	8	9	10	11
12	13	14	15	16	17	18
19	20	21	22	23	24	25
26	27	28	29	30	31	

September 2015

S	M	T	W	T	F	S
		1	2	3	4	5
6	7	8	9	10	11	12
13	14	15	16	17	18	19
20	21	22	23	24	25	26
27	28	29	30			

2015 August

MONDAY
10

TUESDAY
11

WEDNESDAY
12

THURSDAY
13

FRIDAY
14
New Moon

SATURDAY
15

SUNDAY
16

Menus

Grocery

I attribute my success to this—I never gave or took any excuse.

—Florence Nightingale

To Do

July 2015

S	M	T	W	T	F	S
			1	2	3	4
5	6	7	8	9	10	11
12	13	14	15	16	17	18
19	20	21	22	23	24	25
26	27	28	29	30	31	

September 2015

S	M	T	W	T	F	S
		1	2	3	4	5
6	7	8	9	10	11	12
13	14	15	16	17	18	19
20	21	22	23	24	25	26
27	28	29	30			

2015 August

MONDAY
17

TUESDAY
18

WEDNESDAY
19

THURSDAY
20

FRIDAY
21

SATURDAY *First Quarter Moon*
22

SUNDAY
23

Menus

Grocery

You miss 100 percent of the shots you don't take.

—Wayne Gretzky

To Do

July 2015

S	M	T	W	T	F	S
			1	2	3	4
5	6	7	8	9	10	11
12	13	14	15	16	17	18
19	20	21	22	23	24	25
26	27	28	29	30	31	

September 2015

S	M	T	W	T	F	S
		1	2	3	4	5
6	7	8	9	10	11	12
13	14	15	16	17	18	19
20	21	22	23	24	25	26
27	28	29	30			

2015 August

MONDAY
24

TUESDAY
25

WEDNESDAY
26

THURSDAY
27

FRIDAY
28

SATURDAY *Full Moon*
29

SUNDAY
30

Menus

September

SUNDAY	MONDAY	TUESDAY	WEDNESDAY
		1	2
6	7 *Labor Day*	8	9
13 *Rosh Hashanah*	14	15	16
20	21	22 *Yom Kippur*	23 *Autumn begins*
27 *Sukkot*	28	29	30

2015

THURSDAY	FRIDAY	SATURDAY
3	4	5
10	11	12
17	18	19
24	25	26

August 2015

S	M	T	W	T	F	S
						1
2	3	4	5	6	7	8
9	10	11	12	13	14	15
16	17	18	19	20	21	22
23	24	25	26	27	28	29
30	31					

October 2015

S	M	T	W	T	F	S
				1	2	3
4	5	6	7	8	9	10
11	12	13	14	15	16	17
18	19	20	21	22	23	24
25	26	27	28	29	30	31

Monthly Projects

Grocery

The most difficult thing is the decision to act.
The rest is merely tenacity.

—Amelia Earhart

To Do

August 2015

S	M	T	W	T	F	S
						1
2	3	4	5	6	7	8
9	10	11	12	13	14	15
16	17	18	19	20	21	22
23	24	25	26	27	28	29
30	31					

October 2015

S	M	T	W	T	F	S
				1	2	3
4	5	6	7	8	9	10
11	12	13	14	15	16	17
18	19	20	21	22	23	24
25	26	27	28	29	30	31

2015 August/September

MONDAY
31

TUESDAY
1

WEDNESDAY
2

THURSDAY
3

FRIDAY
4

SATURDAY *Last Quarter Moon*
5

SUNDAY
6

Menus

Grocery

Life is what happens to you while you're busy making other plans.

—John Lennon

To Do

August 2015

S	M	T	W	T	F	S
						1
2	3	4	5	6	7	8
9	10	11	12	13	14	15
16	17	18	19	20	21	22
23	24	25	26	27	28	29
30	31					

October 2015

S	M	T	W	T	F	S
				1	2	3
4	5	6	7	8	9	10
11	12	13	14	15	16	17
18	19	20	21	22	23	24
25	26	27	28	29	30	31

2015 September

MONDAY *Labor Day*

7

TUESDAY

8

WEDNESDAY

9

THURSDAY

10

FRIDAY

11

SATURDAY

12

SUNDAY *Rosh Hashanah* *New Moon*

13

Menus

Grocery

We become what we think about.
—Earl Nightingale

To Do

August 2015

S	M	T	W	T	F	S
						1
2	3	4	5	6	7	8
9	10	11	12	13	14	15
16	17	18	19	20	21	22
23	24	25	26	27	28	29
30	31					

October 2015

S	M	T	W	T	F	S
				1	2	3
4	5	6	7	8	9	10
11	12	13	14	15	16	17
18	19	20	21	22	23	24
25	26	27	28	29	30	31

2015 September

MONDAY
14

TUESDAY
15

WEDNESDAY
16

THURSDAY
17

FRIDAY
18

SATURDAY
19

SUNDAY
20

Menus

Grocery

The love of family and the admiration of friends is much more important than wealth and privilege.

—Charles Kuralt

To Do

August 2015

S	M	T	W	T	F	S
						1
2	3	4	5	6	7	8
9	10	11	12	13	14	15
16	17	18	19	20	21	22
23	24	25	26	27	28	29
30	31					

October 2015

S	M	T	W	T	F	S
				1	2	3
4	5	6	7	8	9	10
11	12	13	14	15	16	17
18	19	20	21	22	23	24
25	26	27	28	29	30	31

2015 September

MONDAY *First Quarter Moon*

21

TUESDAY *Yom Kippur*

22

WEDNESDAY *Autumn begins*

23

THURSDAY

24

FRIDAY

25

SATURDAY

26

SUNDAY *Sukkot*

27

Menus

October

SUNDAY	MONDAY	TUESDAY	WEDNESDAY
September 2015 S M T W T F S 1 2 3 4 5 6 7 8 9 10 11 12 13 14 15 16 17 18 19 20 21 22 23 24 25 26 27 28 29 30	November 2015 S M T W T F S 1 2 3 4 5 6 7 8 9 10 11 12 13 14 15 16 17 18 19 20 21 22 23 24 25 26 27 28 29 30		
4	5	6	7
11	12 *Columbus Day Thanksgiving Day (CAN)*	13	14
18	19	20	21
25	26	27	28

2015

THURSDAY	FRIDAY	SATURDAY
1	2	3
8	9	10
15	16	17
22	23	24
29	30	31 *Halloween*

Monthly Projects

Grocery

Life is 10 percent what happens to me and 90 percent how I react to it.

—Charles R. Swindoll

To Do

September 2015

S	M	T	W	T	F	S
		1	2	3	4	5
6	7	8	9	10	11	12
13	14	15	16	17	18	19
20	21	22	23	24	25	26
27	28	29	30			

November 2015

S	M	T	W	T	F	S
1	2	3	4	5	6	7
8	9	10	11	12	13	14
15	16	17	18	19	20	21
22	23	24	25	26	27	28
29	30					

2015 September/October

MONDAY *Full Moon*

28

TUESDAY

29

WEDNESDAY

30

THURSDAY

1

FRIDAY

2

SATURDAY

3

SUNDAY *Last Quarter Moon*

4

Menus

Grocery

The most common way people give up their power is by thinking they don't have any.

—Alice Walker

To Do

September 2015						
S	M	T	W	T	F	S
		1	2	3	4	5
6	7	8	9	10	11	12
13	14	15	16	17	18	19
20	21	22	23	24	25	26
27	28	29	30			

November 2015						
S	M	T	W	T	F	S
1	2	3	4	5	6	7
8	9	10	11	12	13	14
15	16	17	18	19	20	21
22	23	24	25	26	27	28
29	30					

2015 October

MONDAY
5

TUESDAY
6

WEDNESDAY
7

THURSDAY
8

FRIDAY
9

SATURDAY
10

SUNDAY
11

Menus

Grocery

The best time to plant a tree was 20 years ago. The second best time is now.

—Chinese Proverb

To Do

September 2015

S	M	T	W	T	F	S
		1	2	3	4	5
6	7	8	9	10	11	12
13	14	15	16	17	18	19
20	21	22	23	24	25	26
27	28	29	30			

November 2015

S	M	T	W	T	F	S
1	2	3	4	5	6	7
8	9	10	11	12	13	14
15	16	17	18	19	20	21
22	23	24	25	26	27	28
29	30					

2015 October

MONDAY *Columbus Day*
Thanksgiving Day (CAN)
12

TUESDAY *New Moon*
13

WEDNESDAY
14

THURSDAY
15

FRIDAY
16

SATURDAY
17

SUNDAY
18

Menus

Grocery

Your time is limited, so don't waste it living someone else's life.

—Steve Jobs

To Do

September 2015

S	M	T	W	T	F	S
		1	2	3	4	5
6	7	8	9	10	11	12
13	14	15	16	17	18	19
20	21	22	23	24	25	26
27	28	29	30			

November 2015

S	M	T	W	T	F	S
1	2	3	4	5	6	7
8	9	10	11	12	13	14
15	16	17	18	19	20	21
22	23	24	25	26	27	28
29	30					

2015 October

MONDAY
19

TUESDAY
20

First Quarter Moon

WEDNESDAY
21

THURSDAY
22

FRIDAY
23

SATURDAY
24

SUNDAY
25

Menus

November

SUNDAY	MONDAY	TUESDAY	WEDNESDAY
1 *Daylight Saving Time ends*	2	3 *Election Day*	4
8	9	10	11 *Veterans Day Remembrance Day (CAN)*
15	16	17	18
22	23	24	25
29	30		

2015

THURSDAY	FRIDAY	SATURDAY
5	6	7
12	13	14
19	20	21
26 *Thanksgiving Day*	27	28

October 2015

S	M	T	W	T	F	S
				1	2	3
4	5	6	7	8	9	10
11	12	13	14	15	16	17
18	19	20	21	22	23	24
25	26	27	28	29	30	31

December 2015

S	M	T	W	T	F	S
		1	2	3	4	5
6	7	8	9	10	11	12
13	14	15	16	17	18	19
20	21	22	23	24	25	26
27	28	29	30	31		

Monthly Projects

Grocery

I am not a product of my circumstances. I am a product of my decisions.

—Stephen Covey

To Do

September 2015

S	M	T	W	T	F	S
		1	2	3	4	5
6	7	8	9	10	11	12
13	14	15	16	17	18	19
20	21	22	23	24	25	26
27	28	29	30			

November 2015

S	M	T	W	T	F	S
1	2	3	4	5	6	7
8	9	10	11	12	13	14
15	16	17	18	19	20	21
22	23	24	25	26	27	28
29	30					

2015 October/November

MONDAY
26

TUESDAY *Full Moon*
27

WEDNESDAY
28

THURSDAY
29

FRIDAY
30

SATURDAY *Halloween*
31

SUNDAY *Daylight Saving Time ends*
1

Menus

Grocery

You can never cross the ocean until you have the courage to lose sight of the shore.
—Christopher Columbus

To Do

October 2015

S	M	T	W	T	F	S
				1	2	3
4	5	6	7	8	9	10
11	12	13	14	15	16	17
18	19	20	21	22	23	24
25	26	27	28	29	30	31

December 2015

S	M	T	W	T	F	S
		1	2	3	4	5
6	7	8	9	10	11	12
13	14	15	16	17	18	19
20	21	22	23	24	25	26
27	28	29	30	31		

2015 November

MONDAY
2

TUESDAY
3

Election Day
Last Quarter Moon

WEDNESDAY
4

THURSDAY
5

FRIDAY
6

SATURDAY
7

SUNDAY
8

Menus

Grocery

I've learned that people will forget what you said, people will forget what you did, but people will never forget how you made them feel.

—Maya Angelou

To Do

October 2015

S	M	T	W	T	F	S
				1	2	3
4	5	6	7	8	9	10
11	12	13	14	15	16	17
18	19	20	21	22	23	24
25	26	27	28	29	30	31

December 2015

S	M	T	W	T	F	S
		1	2	3	4	5
6	7	8	9	10	11	12
13	14	15	16	17	18	19
20	21	22	23	24	25	26
27	28	29	30	31		

2015 November

MONDAY
9

TUESDAY
10

WEDNESDAY
11

Veterans Day
Remembrance Day (CAN)
New Moon

THURSDAY
12

FRIDAY
13

SATURDAY
14

SUNDAY
15

Menus

Grocery

Either you run the day, or the day runs you.
—Jim Rohn

To Do

October 2015

S	M	T	W	T	F	S
				1	2	3
4	5	6	7	8	9	10
11	12	13	14	15	16	17
18	19	20	21	22	23	24
25	26	27	28	29	30	31

December 2015

S	M	T	W	T	F	S
		1	2	3	4	5
6	7	8	9	10	11	12
13	14	15	16	17	18	19
20	21	22	23	24	25	26
27	28	29	30	31		

2015 November

MONDAY
16

TUESDAY
17

WEDNESDAY
18

THURSDAY *First Quarter Moon*
19

FRIDAY
20

SATURDAY
21

SUNDAY
22

Menus

Grocery

Whether you think you can or you think you can't, you're right.

—Henry Ford

To Do

October 2015

S	M	T	W	T	F	S
				1	2	3
4	5	6	7	8	9	10
11	12	13	14	15	16	17
18	19	20	21	22	23	24
25	26	27	28	29	30	31

December 2015

S	M	T	W	T	F	S
		1	2	3	4	5
6	7	8	9	10	11	12
13	14	15	16	17	18	19
20	21	22	23	24	25	26
27	28	29	30	31		

2015 November

MONDAY
23

TUESDAY
24

WEDNESDAY
25
Full Moon

THURSDAY
26
Thanksgiving Day

FRIDAY
27

SATURDAY
28

SUNDAY
29

Menus

December

SUNDAY	MONDAY	TUESDAY	WEDNESDAY
		1	2
6 *Hanukkah*	7	8	9
13	14	15	16
20	21	22 *Winter begins*	23
27	28	29	30

2015

THURSDAY	FRIDAY	SATURDAY
3	4	5
10	11	12
17	18	19
24 *Christmas Eve*	25 *Christmas Day*	26 *Boxing Day (CAN) Kwanzaa*
31 *New Year's Eve*		

November 2015

S	M	T	W	T	F	S
1	2	3	4	5	6	7
8	9	10	11	12	13	14
15	16	17	18	19	20	21
22	23	24	25	26	27	28
29	30					

January 2016

S	M	T	W	T	F	S
					1	2
3	4	5	6	7	8	9
10	11	12	13	14	15	16
17	18	19	20	21	22	23
24	25	26	27	28	29	30
31						

Monthly Projects

Grocery

The two most important days in your life are the day you are born and the day you find out why.
—Mark Twain

To Do

November 2015

S	M	T	W	T	F	S
1	2	3	4	5	6	7
8	9	10	11	12	13	14
15	16	17	18	19	20	21
22	23	24	25	26	27	28
29	30					

January 2016

S	M	T	W	T	F	S
					1	2
3	4	5	6	7	8	9
10	11	12	13	14	15	16
17	18	19	20	21	22	23
24	25	26	27	28	29	30
31						

2015 November/December

MONDAY
30

TUESDAY
1

WEDNESDAY
2

THURSDAY *Last Quarter Moon*
3

FRIDAY
4

SATURDAY
5

SUNDAY *Hannukah*
6

Menus

Grocery

Life shrinks or expands in proportion to one's courage.

—Anaïs Nin

To Do

November 2015

S	M	T	W	T	F	S
1	2	3	4	5	6	7
8	9	10	11	12	13	14
15	16	17	18	19	20	21
22	23	24	25	26	27	28
29	30					

January 2016

S	M	T	W	T	F	S
					1	2
3	4	5	6	7	8	9
10	11	12	13	14	15	16
17	18	19	20	21	22	23
24	25	26	27	28	29	30
31						

2015 December

MONDAY
7

TUESDAY
8

WEDNESDAY
9

THURSDAY
10

FRIDAY *New Moon*
11

SATURDAY
12

SUNDAY
13

Menus

Grocery

The only person you are destined to become is the person you decide to be.

—Ralph Waldo Emerson

To Do

November 2015

S	M	T	W	T	F	S
1	2	3	4	5	6	7
8	9	10	11	12	13	14
15	16	17	18	19	20	21
22	23	24	25	26	27	28
29	30					

January 2016

S	M	T	W	T	F	S
					1	2
3	4	5	6	7	8	9
10	11	12	13	14	15	16
17	18	19	20	21	22	23
24	25	26	27	28	29	30
31						

2015 December

MONDAY
14

TUESDAY
15

WEDNESDAY
16

THURSDAY
17

FRIDAY
18
First Quarter Moon

SATURDAY
19

SUNDAY
20

Menus

Grocery

If one advances confidently in the direction of his dreams, and endeavors to live the life which he has imagined, he will meet with a success unexpected in common hours.

—Henry David Thoreau

To Do

November 2015

S	M	T	W	T	F	S
1	2	3	4	5	6	7
8	9	10	11	12	13	14
15	16	17	18	19	20	21
22	23	24	25	26	27	28
29	30					

January 2016

S	M	T	W	T	F	S
					1	2
3	4	5	6	7	8	9
10	11	12	13	14	15	16
17	18	19	20	21	22	23
24	25	26	27	28	29	30
31						

2015 December

MONDAY
21

TUESDAY *Winter begins*
22

WEDNESDAY
23

THURSDAY *Christmas Eve*
24

FRIDAY *Christmas Day*
Full Moon
25

SATURDAY *Boxing Day (CAN)*
Kwanzaa
26

SUNDAY
27

Menus

January

SUNDAY	MONDAY	TUESDAY	WEDNESDAY
December 2015 S M T W T F S 1 2 3 4 5 6 7 8 9 10 11 12 13 14 15 16 17 18 19 20 21 22 23 24 25 26 27 28 29 30 31	February 2016 S M T W T F S 1 2 3 4 5 6 7 8 9 10 11 12 13 14 15 16 17 18 19 20 21 22 23 24 25 26 27 28 29		
3	4	5	6
10	11	12	13
17	18 *Martin Luther King, Jr. Day*	19	20
24 / 31	25	26	27

2016

THURSDAY	FRIDAY	SATURDAY
	1 *New Year's Day*	2
7	8	9
14	15	16
21	22	23
28	29	30

Monthly Projects

Grocery

When I stand before God at the end of my life, I would hope that I would not have a single bit of talent left and could say, "I used everything you gave me."

—Erma Bombeck

To Do

December 2015

S	M	T	W	T	F	S
		1	2	3	4	5
6	7	8	9	10	11	12
13	14	15	16	17	18	19
20	21	22	23	24	25	26
27	28	29	30	31		

February 2016

S	M	T	W	T	F	S
	1	2	3	4	5	6
7	8	9	10	11	12	13
14	15	16	17	18	19	20
21	22	23	24	25	26	27
28	29					

2015/
2016

December/January

MONDAY
28

TUESDAY
29

WEDNESDAY
30

THURSDAY *New Year's Eve*
31

FRIDAY *New Year's Day*
1

SATURDAY *Last Quarter Moon*
2

SUNDAY
3

Menus

Grocery

Certain things catch your eye, but pursue only those that capture the heart.

—Native American Proverb

To Do

December 2015

S	M	T	W	T	F	S
		1	2	3	4	5
6	7	8	9	10	11	12
13	14	15	16	17	18	19
20	21	22	23	24	25	26
27	28	29	30	31		

February 2016

S	M	T	W	T	F	S
	1	2	3	4	5	6
7	8	9	10	11	12	13
14	15	16	17	18	19	20
21	22	23	24	25	26	27
28	29					

2016 January

MONDAY
4

TUESDAY
5

WEDNESDAY
6

THURSDAY
7

FRIDAY
8

SATURDAY
9

SUNDAY *New Moon*
10

Menus

Grocery

Believe you can and you're halfway there.
—Theodore Roosevelt

To Do

December 2015

S	M	T	W	T	F	S
		1	2	3	4	5
6	7	8	9	10	11	12
13	14	15	16	17	18	19
20	21	22	23	24	25	26
27	28	29	30	31		

February 2016

S	M	T	W	T	F	S
	1	2	3	4	5	6
7	8	9	10	11	12	13
14	15	16	17	18	19	20
21	22	23	24	25	26	27
28	29					

2016 January

MONDAY
11

TUESDAY
12

WEDNESDAY
13

THURSDAY
14 no one + nothing

FRIDAY
15

SATURDAY *First Quarter Moon*
16

SUNDAY
17

Menus

Grocery

Everything you've ever wanted is on the other side of fear.

—George Addair

To Do

December 2015

S	M	T	W	T	F	S
		1	2	3	4	5
6	7	8	9	10	11	12
13	14	15	16	17	18	19
20	21	22	23	24	25	26
27	28	29	30	31		

February 2016

S	M	T	W	T	F	S
	1	2	3	4	5	6
7	8	9	10	11	12	13
14	15	16	17	18	19	20
21	22	23	24	25	26	27
28	29					

2016 January

MONDAY *Martin Luther King, Jr. Day*

18

TUESDAY

19

WEDNESDAY

20

THURSDAY

21

FRIDAY

22

SATURDAY

23

SUNDAY *Full Moon*

24

Menus

Grocery

Start where you are. Use what you have. Do what you can.

—Arthur Ashe

To Do

December 2015

S	M	T	W	T	F	S
		1	2	3	4	5
6	7	8	9	10	11	12
13	14	15	16	17	18	19
20	21	22	23	24	25	26
27	28	29	30	31		

February 2016

S	M	T	W	T	F	S
	1	2	3	4	5	6
7	8	9	10	11	12	13
14	15	16	17	18	19	20
21	22	23	24	25	26	27
28	29					

2016 January

MONDAY
25

TUESDAY
26

WEDNESDAY
27

THURSDAY
28

FRIDAY
29

SATURDAY
30

SUNDAY
31

Menus

February

SUNDAY	MONDAY	TUESDAY	WEDNESDAY
	1	2 *Groundhog Day*	3
7	8 *Chinese New Year*	9	10 *Ash Wednesday (Lent begins)*
14 *Valentine's Day*	15 *Presidents' Day*	16	17
21	22 *George Washington's Birthday*	23	24
28	29		

2016

THURSDAY	FRIDAY	SATURDAY
4	5	6
11	12 *Abraham Lincoln's Birthday*	13
18	19	20
25	26	27

January 2016

S	M	T	W	T	F	S
					1	2
3	4	5	6	7	8	9
10	11	12	13	14	15	16
17	18	19	20	21	22	23
24	25	26	27	28	29	30
31						

March 2016

S	M	T	W	T	F	S
		1	2	3	4	5
6	7	8	9	10	11	12
13	14	15	16	17	18	19
20	21	22	23	24	25	26
27	28	29	30	31		

Monthly Projects

Grocery

Fall seven times and stand up eight.
—Japanese Proverb

To Do

January 2016

S	M	T	W	T	F	S
					1	2
3	4	5	6	7	8	9
10	11	12	13	14	15	16
17	18	19	20	21	22	23
24	25	26	27	28	29	30
31						

March 2016

S	M	T	W	T	F	S
		1	2	3	4	5
6	7	8	9	10	11	12
13	14	15	16	17	18	19
20	21	22	23	24	25	26
27	28	29	30	31		

2016 February

MONDAY *Last Quarter Moon*

1

TUESDAY *Groundhog Day*

2

WEDNESDAY

3

THURSDAY

4

FRIDAY

5

SATURDAY

6

SUNDAY

7

Menus

Grocery

When one door of happiness closes, another opens, but often we look so long at the closed door that we do not see the one that has been opened for us.

—Helen Keller

To Do

January 2016

S	M	T	W	T	F	S
					1	2
3	4	5	6	7	8	9
10	11	12	13	14	15	16
17	18	19	20	21	22	23
24	25	26	27	28	29	30
31						

March 2016

S	M	T	W	T	F	S
		1	2	3	4	5
6	7	8	9	10	11	12
13	14	15	16	17	18	19
20	21	22	23	24	25	26
27	28	29	30	31		

2016 February

MONDAY *Chinese New Year*
New Moon
8

TUESDAY
9

WEDNESDAY *Ash Wednesday (Lent begins)*
10

THURSDAY
11

FRIDAY *Abraham Lincoln's Birthday*
12

SATURDAY
13

SUNDAY *Valentine's Day*
14

Menus

Grocery

When I let go of what I am, I become what I might be.

—Lao Tzu

To Do

January 2016

S	M	T	W	T	F	S
					1	2
3	4	5	6	7	8	9
10	11	12	13	14	15	16
17	18	19	20	21	22	23
24	25	26	27	28	29	30
31						

March 2016

S	M	T	W	T	F	S
		1	2	3	4	5
6	7	8	9	10	11	12
13	14	15	16	17	18	19
20	21	22	23	24	25	26
27	28	29	30	31		

2016 February

MONDAY
15

Presidents' Day
First Quarter Moon

TUESDAY
16

WEDNESDAY
17

THURSDAY
18

FRIDAY
19

SATURDAY
20

SUNDAY
21

Menus

Grocery

Family is not an important thing. It's everything.
—Michael J. Fox

To Do

January 2016

S	M	T	W	T	F	S
					1	2
3	4	5	6	7	8	9
10	11	12	13	14	15	16
17	18	19	20	21	22	23
24	25	26	27	28	29	30
31						

March 2016

S	M	T	W	T	F	S
		1	2	3	4	5
6	7	8	9	10	11	12
13	14	15	16	17	18	19
20	21	22	23	24	25	26
27	28	29	30	31		

2016 February

MONDAY
22

George Washington's Birthday
Full Moon

TUESDAY
23

WEDNESDAY
24

THURSDAY
25

FRIDAY
26

SATURDAY
27

SUNDAY
28

Menus

March

SUNDAY	MONDAY	TUESDAY	WEDNESDAY
		1	2
6	7	8 *International Women's Day*	9
13 *Daylight Saving Time begins*	14 *Commonwealth Day (CAN)*	15	16
20 *Spring begins Palm Sunday*	21	22	23 *Purim*
27 *Easter*	28 *Easter Monday (CAN)*	29	30

2016

THURSDAY	FRIDAY	SATURDAY
3	4	5
10	11	12
17 *St. Patrick's Day*	18	19
24	25 *Good Friday*	26
31		

February 2016

S	M	T	W	T	F	S
	1	2	3	4	5	6
7	8	9	10	11	12	13
14	15	16	17	18	19	20
21	22	23	24	25	26	27
28	29					

April 2016

S	M	T	W	T	F	S
					1	2
3	4	5	6	7	8	9
10	11	12	13	14	15	16
17	18	19	20	21	22	23
24	25	26	27	28	29	30

Monthly Projects

Grocery

Happiness is not something readymade. It comes from your own actions.

—Dalai Lama

To Do

February 2016

S	M	T	W	T	F	S
	1	2	3	4	5	6
7	8	9	10	11	12	13
14	15	16	17	18	19	20
21	22	23	24	25	26	27
28	29					

April 2016

S	M	T	W	T	F	S
					1	2
3	4	5	6	7	8	9
10	11	12	13	14	15	16
17	18	19	20	21	22	23
24	25	26	27	28	29	30

2016 February/March

MONDAY
29

TUESDAY
Last Quarter Moon
1

WEDNESDAY
2

THURSDAY
3

FRIDAY
4

SATURDAY
5

SUNDAY
6

Menus

Grocery

You can't fall if you don't climb. But there's no joy in living your whole life on the ground.
—Anonymous

To Do

February 2016

S	M	T	W	T	F	S
	1	2	3	4	5	6
7	8	9	10	11	12	13
14	15	16	17	18	19	20
21	22	23	24	25	26	27
28	29					

April 2016

S	M	T	W	T	F	S
					1	2
3	4	5	6	7	8	9
10	11	12	13	14	15	16
17	18	19	20	21	22	23
24	25	26	27	28	29	30

2016 March

MONDAY
7

TUESDAY *International Women's Day*
8

WEDNESDAY *New Moon*
9

THURSDAY
10

FRIDAY
11

SATURDAY
12

SUNDAY *Daylight Saving Time begins*
13

Menus

Grocery

Too many of us are not living our dreams because we are living our fears.

—Les Brown

To Do

February 2016

S	M	T	W	T	F	S
	1	2	3	4	5	6
7	8	9	10	11	12	13
14	15	16	17	18	19	20
21	22	23	24	25	26	27
28	29					

April 2016

S	M	T	W	T	F	S
					1	2
3	4	5	6	7	8	9
10	11	12	13	14	15	16
17	18	19	20	21	22	23
24	25	26	27	28	29	30

2016 March

MONDAY *Commonwealth Day (CAN)*

14

TUESDAY *First Quarter Moon*

15

WEDNESDAY

16

THURSDAY *St. Patrick's Day*

17

FRIDAY

18

SATURDAY

19

SUNDAY *Spring begins*
Palm Sunday

20

Menus

Grocery

Challenges are what make life interesting; overcoming them is what makes life meaningful.

—Joshua J. Marine

To Do

February 2016

S	M	T	W	T	F	S
	1	2	3	4	5	6
7	8	9	10	11	12	13
14	15	16	17	18	19	20
21	22	23	24	25	26	27
28	29					

April 2016

S	M	T	W	T	F	S
					1	2
3	4	5	6	7	8	9
10	11	12	13	14	15	16
17	18	19	20	21	22	23
24	25	26	27	28	29	30

2016 March

MONDAY
21

TUESDAY
22

WEDNESDAY
23
Purim
Full Moon

THURSDAY
24

FRIDAY
25
Good Friday

SATURDAY
26

SUNDAY
27
Easter

Menus

April

SUNDAY	MONDAY	TUESDAY	WEDNESDAY
March 2016 S M T W T F S 1 2 3 4 5 6 7 8 9 10 11 12 13 14 15 16 17 18 19 20 21 22 23 24 25 26 27 28 29 30 31	May 2016 S M T W T F S 1 2 3 4 5 6 7 8 9 10 11 12 13 14 15 16 17 18 19 20 21 22 23 24 25 26 27 28 29 30 31		
3	4	5	6
10	11	12	13
17	18	19	20
24	25	26	27

2016

THURSDAY	FRIDAY	SATURDAY
	1 *April Fools' Day*	2
7	8	9
14	15	16
21	22 *Earth Day* *Passover*	23
28	29	30

Monthly Projects

Grocery

If you want to lift yourself up, lift up someone else.

—Booker T. Washington

To Do

March 2016

S	M	T	W	T	F	S
		1	2	3	4	5
6	7	8	9	10	11	12
13	14	15	16	17	18	19
20	21	22	23	24	25	26
27	28	29	30	31		

May 2016

S	M	T	W	T	F	S
1	2	3	4	5	6	7
8	9	10	11	12	13	14
15	16	17	18	19	20	21
22	23	24	25	26	27	28
29	30	31				

2016 March/April

MONDAY *Easter Monday (CAN)*

28

TUESDAY

29

WEDNESDAY

30

THURSDAY *Last Quarter Moon*

31

FRIDAY *April Fools' Day*

1

SATURDAY

2

SUNDAY

3

Menus

Grocery

Limitations live only in our minds. But if we use our imaginations, our possibilities become limitless.

—Jamie Paolinetti

To Do

March 2016

S	M	T	W	T	F	S
		1	2	3	4	5
6	7	8	9	10	11	12
13	14	15	16	17	18	19
20	21	22	23	24	25	26
27	28	29	30	31		

May 2016

S	M	T	W	T	F	S
1	2	3	4	5	6	7
8	9	10	11	12	13	14
15	16	17	18	19	20	21
22	23	24	25	26	27	28
29	30	31				

2016 April

MONDAY
4

TUESDAY
5

WEDNESDAY
6

THURSDAY
7

New Moon

FRIDAY
8

SATURDAY
9

SUNDAY
10

Menus

Grocery

I didn't fail the test. I just found 100 ways to do it wrong.

—Benjamin Franklin

To Do

March 2016

S	M	T	W	T	F	S
		1	2	3	4	5
6	7	8	9	10	11	12
13	14	15	16	17	18	19
20	21	22	23	24	25	26
27	28	29	30	31		

May 2016

S	M	T	W	T	F	S
1	2	3	4	5	6	7
8	9	10	11	12	13	14
15	16	17	18	19	20	21
22	23	24	25	26	27	28
29	30	31				

2016 April

MONDAY
11

TUESDAY
12

WEDNESDAY
13

THURSDAY
14
First Quarter Moon

FRIDAY
15

SATURDAY
16

SUNDAY
17

Menus

Grocery

In order to succeed, your desire for success should be greater than your fear of failure.
—Bill Cosby

To Do

March 2016

S	M	T	W	T	F	S
		1	2	3	4	5
6	7	8	9	10	11	12
13	14	15	16	17	18	19
20	21	22	23	24	25	26
27	28	29	30	31		

May 2016

S	M	T	W	T	F	S
1	2	3	4	5	6	7
8	9	10	11	12	13	14
15	16	17	18	19	20	21
22	23	24	25	26	27	28
29	30	31				

2016 April

MONDAY
18

TUESDAY
19

WEDNESDAY
20

THURSDAY
21

FRIDAY
22

Earth Day
Passover
Full Moon

SATURDAY
23

SUNDAY
24

Menus

Grocery

A person who never made a mistake never tried anything new.

— Albert Einstein

To Do

March 2016

S	M	T	W	T	F	S
		1	2	3	4	5
6	7	8	9	10	11	12
13	14	15	16	17	18	19
20	21	22	23	24	25	26
27	28	29	30	31		

May 2016

S	M	T	W	T	F	S
1	2	3	4	5	6	7
8	9	10	11	12	13	14
15	16	17	18	19	20	21
22	23	24	25	26	27	28
29	30	31				

2016 April/May

MONDAY
25

TUESDAY
26

WEDNESDAY
27

THURSDAY
28

FRIDAY
29

SATURDAY *Last Quarter Moon*
30

SUNDAY
1

Menus

May

SUNDAY	MONDAY	TUESDAY	WEDNESDAY
1	2	3	4
8 *Mother's Day*	9	10	11
15	16	17	18
22	23 *Victoria Day (CAN)*	24	25
29	30 *Memorial Day*	31	

2016

THURSDAY	FRIDAY	SATURDAY
5 *Cinco de Mayo*	6	7
12	13	14
19	20	21 *Armed Forces Day*
26	27	28
	April 2016	June 2016

April 2016

S	M	T	W	T	F	S
					1	2
3	4	5	6	7	8	9
10	11	12	13	14	15	16
17	18	19	20	21	22	23
24	25	26	27	28	29	30

June 2016

S	M	T	W	T	F	S
			1	2	3	4
5	6	7	8	9	10	11
12	13	14	15	16	17	18
19	20	21	22	23	24	25
26	27	28	29	30		

Monthly Projects

Grocery

The person who says it cannot be done should not interrupt the person who is doing it.
—Chinese Proverb

To Do

April 2016

S	M	T	W	T	F	S
					1	2
3	4	5	6	7	8	9
10	11	12	13	14	15	16
17	18	19	20	21	22	23
24	25	26	27	28	29	30

June 2016

S	M	T	W	T	F	S
			1	2	3	4
5	6	7	8	9	10	11
12	13	14	15	16	17	18
19	20	21	22	23	24	25
26	27	28	29	30		

2016 May

MONDAY
2

TUESDAY
3

WEDNESDAY
4

THURSDAY *Cinco de Mayo*
5

FRIDAY *New Moon*
6

SATURDAY
7

SUNDAY *Mother's Day*
8

Menus

Grocery

There are no traffic jams along the extra mile.

—Roger Staubach

To Do

April 2016

S	M	T	W	T	F	S
					1	2
3	4	5	6	7	8	9
10	11	12	13	14	15	16
17	18	19	20	21	22	23
24	25	26	27	28	29	30

June 2016

S	M	T	W	T	F	S
			1	2	3	4
5	6	7	8	9	10	11
12	13	14	15	16	17	18
19	20	21	22	23	24	25
26	27	28	29	30		

2016 May

MONDAY
9

TUESDAY
10

WEDNESDAY
11

THURSDAY
12

FRIDAY
13
First Quarter Moon

SATURDAY
14

SUNDAY
15

Menus

Grocery

I think togetherness is a very important ingredient to family life.

—Barbara Bush

To Do

April 2016

S	M	T	W	T	F	S
					1	2
3	4	5	6	7	8	9
10	11	12	13	14	15	16
17	18	19	20	21	22	23
24	25	26	27	28	29	30

June 2016

S	M	T	W	T	F	S
			1	2	3	4
5	6	7	8	9	10	11
12	13	14	15	16	17	18
19	20	21	22	23	24	25
26	27	28	29	30		

2016 May

MONDAY
16

TUESDAY
17

WEDNESDAY
18

THURSDAY
19

FRIDAY
20

SATURDAY
21

Armed Forces Day
Full Moon

SUNDAY
22

Menus

Grocery

Some of the most important conversations I've ever had occurred at my family's dinner table.
—Bob Ehrlich

To Do

April 2016

S	M	T	W	T	F	S
					1	2
3	4	5	6	7	8	9
10	11	12	13	14	15	16
17	18	19	20	21	22	23
24	25	26	27	28	29	30

June 2016

S	M	T	W	T	F	S
			1	2	3	4
5	6	7	8	9	10	11
12	13	14	15	16	17	18
19	20	21	22	23	24	25
26	27	28	29	30		

2016 May

MONDAY *Victoria Day (CAN)*

23

TUESDAY

24

WEDNESDAY

25

THURSDAY

26

FRIDAY

27

SATURDAY

28

SUNDAY *Last Quarter Moon*

29

Menus

June

SUNDAY	MONDAY	TUESDAY	WEDNESDAY
			1
5	6 *Ramadan*	7	8
12	13	14 *Flag Day*	15
19 *Father's Day*	20 *Summer begins*	21	22
26	27	28	29

2016

THURSDAY	FRIDAY	SATURDAY
2	3	4
9	10	11 *Shavuot*
16	17	18
23	24	25
30		

May 2016

S	M	T	W	T	F	S
1	2	3	4	5	6	7
8	9	10	11	12	13	14
15	16	17	18	19	20	21
22	23	24	25	26	27	28
29	30	31				

July 2016

S	M	T	W	T	F	S
					1	2
3	4	5	6	7	8	9
10	11	12	13	14	15	16
17	18	19	20	21	22	23
24	25	26	27	28	29	30
31						

Monthly Projects

Grocery

To be yourself in a world that is constantly trying to make you something else is the greatest accomplishment.

—Ralph Waldo Emerson

To Do

May 2016

S	M	T	W	T	F	S
1	2	3	4	5	6	7
8	9	10	11	12	13	14
15	16	17	18	19	20	21
22	23	24	25	26	27	28
29	30	31				

July 2016

S	M	T	W	T	F	S
					1	2
3	4	5	6	7	8	9
10	11	12	13	14	15	16
17	18	19	20	21	22	23
24	25	26	27	28	29	30
31						

2016 May/June

MONDAY — *Memorial Day*

30

TUESDAY

31

WEDNESDAY

1

THURSDAY

2

FRIDAY

3

SATURDAY

4

SUNDAY — *New Moon*

5

Menus

Grocery

It is better to remain silent at the risk of being thought a fool, than to talk and remove all doubt of it.

—Maurice Switzer

To Do

May 2016

S	M	T	W	T	F	S
1	2	3	4	5	6	7
8	9	10	11	12	13	14
15	16	17	18	19	20	21
22	23	24	25	26	27	28
29	30	31				

July 2016

S	M	T	W	T	F	S
					1	2
3	4	5	6	7	8	9
10	11	12	13	14	15	16
17	18	19	20	21	22	23
24	25	26	27	28	29	30
31						

2016 June

MONDAY *Ramadan*
6

TUESDAY
7

WEDNESDAY
8

THURSDAY
9

FRIDAY
10

SATURDAY *Shavuot*
11

SUNDAY *First Quarter Moon*
12

Menus

Grocery

There are only two ways to live your life. One is as though nothing is a miracle. The other is as though everything is a miracle.

—Albert Einstein

To Do

May 2016

S	M	T	W	T	F	S
1	2	3	4	5	6	7
8	9	10	11	12	13	14
15	16	17	18	19	20	21
22	23	24	25	26	27	28
29	30	31				

July 2016

S	M	T	W	T	F	S
					1	2
3	4	5	6	7	8	9
10	11	12	13	14	15	16
17	18	19	20	21	22	23
24	25	26	27	28	29	30
31						

2016 June

MONDAY
13

TUESDAY — *Flag Day*
14

WEDNESDAY
15

THURSDAY
16

FRIDAY
17

SATURDAY
18

SUNDAY — *Father's Day*
19

Menus

Grocery

If you don't stand for something, you will fall for anything.

—Gordon A. Eadie

To Do

May 2016

S	M	T	W	T	F	S
1	2	3	4	5	6	7
8	9	10	11	12	13	14
15	16	17	18	19	20	21
22	23	24	25	26	27	28
29	30	31				

July 2016

S	M	T	W	T	F	S
					1	2
3	4	5	6	7	8	9
10	11	12	13	14	15	16
17	18	19	20	21	22	23
24	25	26	27	28	29	30
31						

2016 June

MONDAY

20

Summer begins
Full Moon

TUESDAY

21

WEDNESDAY

22

THURSDAY

23

FRIDAY

24

SATURDAY

25

SUNDAY

26

Menus

July

SUNDAY	MONDAY	TUESDAY	WEDNESDAY
June 2016 S M T W T F S 1 2 3 4 5 6 7 8 9 10 11 12 13 14 15 16 17 18 19 20 21 22 23 24 25 26 27 28 29 30	August 2016 S M T W T F S 1 2 3 4 5 6 7 8 9 10 11 12 13 14 15 16 17 18 19 20 21 22 23 24 25 26 27 28 29 30 31		
3	4 *Independence Day*	5	6
10	11	12	13
17	18	19	20
24 / 31	25	26	27

2016

THURSDAY	FRIDAY	SATURDAY
	1 *Canada Day (CAN)*	2
7	8	9
14	15	16
21	22	23
28	29	30

Monthly Projects

Grocery

Most of the shadows of this life are caused by our standing in our own sunshine.
—Ralph Waldo Emerson

To Do

June 2016

S	M	T	W	T	F	S
			1	2	3	4
5	6	7	8	9	10	11
12	13	14	15	16	17	18
19	20	21	22	23	24	25
26	27	28	29	30		

August 2016

S	M	T	W	T	F	S
	1	2	3	4	5	6
7	8	9	10	11	12	13
14	15	16	17	18	19	20
21	22	23	24	25	26	27
28	29	30	31			

2016 June/July

MONDAY *Last Quarter Moon*

27

TUESDAY

28

WEDNESDAY

29

THURSDAY

30

FRIDAY *Canada Day (CAN)*

1

SATURDAY

2

SUNDAY

3

Menus

Grocery

Life isn't a matter of milestones, but of moments.
—Rose Kennedy

To Do

June 2016

S	M	T	W	T	F	S
			1	2	3	4
5	6	7	8	9	10	11
12	13	14	15	16	17	18
19	20	21	22	23	24	25
26	27	28	29	30		

August 2016

S	M	T	W	T	F	S
	1	2	3	4	5	6
7	8	9	10	11	12	13
14	15	16	17	18	19	20
21	22	23	24	25	26	27
28	29	30	31			

2016 July

MONDAY *Independence Day*
New Moon

4

TUESDAY

5

WEDNESDAY

6

THURSDAY

7

FRIDAY

8

SATURDAY

9

SUNDAY

10

Menus

Grocery

Happiness is not a goal, but a by-product.
—Eleanor Roosevelt

To Do

June 2016

S	M	T	W	T	F	S
			1	2	3	4
5	6	7	8	9	10	11
12	13	14	15	16	17	18
19	20	21	22	23	24	25
26	27	28	29	30		

August 2016

S	M	T	W	T	F	S
	1	2	3	4	5	6
7	8	9	10	11	12	13
14	15	16	17	18	19	20
21	22	23	24	25	26	27
28	29	30	31			

2016 July

MONDAY
11

TUESDAY *First Quarter Moon*
12

WEDNESDAY
13

THURSDAY
14

FRIDAY
15

SATURDAY
16

SUNDAY
17

Menus

Grocery

Happiness is where we find it, but rarely where we seek it.

—J. Petit-Senn

To Do

June 2016

S	M	T	W	T	F	S
			1	2	3	4
5	6	7	8	9	10	11
12	13	14	15	16	17	18
19	20	21	22	23	24	25
26	27	28	29	30		

August 2016

S	M	T	W	T	F	S
	1	2	3	4	5	6
7	8	9	10	11	12	13
14	15	16	17	18	19	20
21	22	23	24	25	26	27
28	29	30	31			

2016 July

MONDAY
18

TUESDAY *Full Moon*
19

WEDNESDAY
20

THURSDAY
21

FRIDAY
22

SATURDAY
23

SUNDAY
24

Menus

Grocery

The art of being wise is knowing what to overlook.

—William James

To Do

June 2016

S	M	T	W	T	F	S
			1	2	3	4
5	6	7	8	9	10	11
12	13	14	15	16	17	18
19	20	21	22	23	24	25
26	27	28	29	30		

August 2016

S	M	T	W	T	F	S
	1	2	3	4	5	6
7	8	9	10	11	12	13
14	15	16	17	18	19	20
21	22	23	24	25	26	27
28	29	30	31			

2016 July

MONDAY
25

TUESDAY *Last Quarter Moon*
26

WEDNESDAY
27

THURSDAY
28

FRIDAY
29

SATURDAY
30

SUNDAY
31

Menus

August

SUNDAY	MONDAY	TUESDAY	WEDNESDAY
	1 *Civic Holiday (CAN)*	2	3
7	8	9	10
14	15	16	17
21	22	23	24
28	29	30	31

2016

THURSDAY	FRIDAY	SATURDAY
4	5	6
11	12	13
18	19	20
25	26	27

July 2016

S	M	T	W	T	F	S
					1	2
3	4	5	6	7	8	9
10	11	12	13	14	15	16
17	18	19	20	21	22	23
24	25	26	27	28	29	30
31						

September 2016

S	M	T	W	T	F	S
				1	2	3
4	5	6	7	8	9	10
11	12	13	14	15	16	17
18	19	20	21	22	23	24
25	26	27	28	29	30	

Monthly Projects

Grocery

Nothing great was ever achieved without enthusiasm.

—Ralph Waldo Emerson

To Do

July 2016

S	M	T	W	T	F	S
					1	2
3	4	5	6	7	8	9
10	11	12	13	14	15	16
17	18	19	20	21	22	23
24	25	26	27	28	29	30
31						

September 2016

S	M	T	W	T	F	S
				1	2	3
4	5	6	7	8	9	10
11	12	13	14	15	16	17
18	19	20	21	22	23	24
25	26	27	28	29	30	

2016 August

MONDAY *Civic Holiday (CAN)*

1

TUESDAY *New Moon*

2

WEDNESDAY

3

THURSDAY

4

FRIDAY

5

SATURDAY

6

SUNDAY

7

Menus

Grocery

You must be the change you wish to see in the world.

—Mahatma Gandhi

To Do

July 2016

S	M	T	W	T	F	S
					1	2
3	4	5	6	7	8	9
10	11	12	13	14	15	16
17	18	19	20	21	22	23
24	25	26	27	28	29	30
31						

September 2016

S	M	T	W	T	F	S
				1	2	3
4	5	6	7	8	9	10
11	12	13	14	15	16	17
18	19	20	21	22	23	24
25	26	27	28	29	30	

2016 August

MONDAY
8

TUESDAY
9

WEDNESDAY *First Quarter Moon*
10

THURSDAY
11

FRIDAY
12

SATURDAY
13

SUNDAY
14

Menus

Grocery

The shortest way to do many things is to do only one thing at a time.

—Richard Cech

To Do

July 2016

S	M	T	W	T	F	S
					1	2
3	4	5	6	7	8	9
10	11	12	13	14	15	16
17	18	19	20	21	22	23
24	25	26	27	28	29	30
31						

September 2016

S	M	T	W	T	F	S
				1	2	3
4	5	6	7	8	9	10
11	12	13	14	15	16	17
18	19	20	21	22	23	24
25	26	27	28	29	30	

2016 August

MONDAY
15

TUESDAY
16

WEDNESDAY
17

THURSDAY
Full Moon
18

FRIDAY
19

SATURDAY
20

SUNDAY
21

Menus

Grocery

Those that make the best use of their time have none to spare.

—Thomas Fuller

To Do

July 2016

S	M	T	W	T	F	S
					1	2
3	4	5	6	7	8	9
10	11	12	13	14	15	16
17	18	19	20	21	22	23
24	25	26	27	28	29	30
31						

September 2016

S	M	T	W	T	F	S
				1	2	3
4	5	6	7	8	9	10
11	12	13	14	15	16	17
18	19	20	21	22	23	24
25	26	27	28	29	30	

2016 August

MONDAY
22

TUESDAY
23

WEDNESDAY
24

THURSDAY
25
Last Quarter Moon

FRIDAY
26

SATURDAY
27

SUNDAY
28

Menus

September

SUNDAY	MONDAY	TUESDAY	WEDNESDAY
August 2016 S M T W T F S 1 2 3 4 5 6 7 8 9 10 11 12 13 14 15 16 17 18 19 20 21 22 23 24 25 26 27 28 29 30 31	October 2016 S M T W T F S 1 2 3 4 5 6 7 8 9 10 11 12 13 14 15 16 17 18 19 20 21 22 23 24 25 26 27 28 29 30 31		
4	5 *Labor Day*	6	7
11	12	13	14
18	19	20	21
25	26	27	28

2016

THURSDAY	FRIDAY	SATURDAY
1	2	3
8	9	10
15	16	17
22 *Autumn begins*	23	24
29	30	

Monthly Projects

Grocery

Persistent people begin their success where others end in failure.

—Edward Eggleston

To Do

August 2016

S	M	T	W	T	F	S
	1	2	3	4	5	6
7	8	9	10	11	12	13
14	15	16	17	18	19	20
21	22	23	24	25	26	27
28	29	30	31			

October 2016

S	M	T	W	T	F	S
						1
2	3	4	5	6	7	8
9	10	11	12	13	14	15
16	17	18	19	20	21	22
23	24	25	26	27	28	29
30	31					

2016 August/September

MONDAY
29

TUESDAY
30

WEDNESDAY
31

THURSDAY *New Moon*
1

FRIDAY
2

SATURDAY
3

SUNDAY
4

Menus

Grocery

Great works are performed not by strength, but by perseverance.

—Samuel Johnson

To Do

August 2016

S	M	T	W	T	F	S
	1	2	3	4	5	6
7	8	9	10	11	12	13
14	15	16	17	18	19	20
21	22	23	24	25	26	27
28	29	30	31			

October 2016

S	M	T	W	T	F	S
						1
2	3	4	5	6	7	8
9	10	11	12	13	14	15
16	17	18	19	20	21	22
23	24	25	26	27	28	29
30	31					

2016 September

MONDAY *Labor Day*

5

TUESDAY

6

WEDNESDAY

7

THURSDAY

8

FRIDAY *First Quarter Moon*

9

SATURDAY

10

SUNDAY

11

Menus

Grocery

Opportunity is missed by most people because it is dressed in overalls and looks like work.
—Thomas A. Edison

To Do

August 2016

S	M	T	W	T	F	S
	1	2	3	4	5	6
7	8	9	10	11	12	13
14	15	16	17	18	19	20
21	22	23	24	25	26	27
28	29	30	31			

October 2016

S	M	T	W	T	F	S
						1
2	3	4	5	6	7	8
9	10	11	12	13	14	15
16	17	18	19	20	21	22
23	24	25	26	27	28	29
30	31					

2016 September

MONDAY
12

TUESDAY
13

WEDNESDAY
14

THURSDAY
15

FRIDAY
16
Full Moon

SATURDAY
17

SUNDAY
18

Menus

Grocery

You must look into other people as well as at them.

—Lord Chesterfield

To Do

August 2016

S	M	T	W	T	F	S
	1	2	3	4	5	6
7	8	9	10	11	12	13
14	15	16	17	18	19	20
21	22	23	24	25	26	27
28	29	30	31			

October 2016

S	M	T	W	T	F	S
						1
2	3	4	5	6	7	8
9	10	11	12	13	14	15
16	17	18	19	20	21	22
23	24	25	26	27	28	29
30	31					

2016 September

MONDAY
19

TUESDAY
20

WEDNESDAY
21

THURSDAY
22
Autumn begins

FRIDAY
23
Last Quarter Moon

SATURDAY
24

SUNDAY
25

Menus

October

SUNDAY	MONDAY	TUESDAY	WEDNESDAY
September 2016 S M T W T F S 1 2 3 4 5 6 7 8 9 10 11 12 13 14 15 16 17 18 19 20 21 22 23 24 25 26 27 28 29 30	November 2016 S M T W T F S 1 2 3 4 5 6 7 8 9 10 11 12 13 14 15 16 17 18 19 20 21 22 23 24 25 26 27 28 29 30		
2 *Rosh Hashanah*	3	4	5
9	10 *Columbus Day Thanksgiving Day (CAN)*	11 *Yom Kippur*	12
16 *Sukkot*	17	18	19
23 / 30	24 / *Halloween* 31	25	26

2016

THURSDAY	FRIDAY	SATURDAY
		1
6	7	8
13	14	15
20	21	22
27	28	29

Monthly Projects

Grocery

Kind words are the music of the world.
—F. W. Faber

To Do

September 2016

S	M	T	W	T	F	S
				1	2	3
4	5	6	7	8	9	10
11	12	13	14	15	16	17
18	19	20	21	22	23	24
25	26	27	28	29	30	

November 2016

S	M	T	W	T	F	S
		1	2	3	4	5
6	7	8	9	10	11	12
13	14	15	16	17	18	19
20	21	22	23	24	25	26
27	28	29	30			

2016 September/October

MONDAY
26

TUESDAY
27

WEDNESDAY
28

THURSDAY
29

FRIDAY
30

SATURDAY *New Moon*
1

SUNDAY *Rosh Hashanah*
2

Menus

Grocery

Effort only fully releases its reward after a person refuses to quit.

—Napoleon Hill

To Do

September 2016

S	M	T	W	T	F	S
				1	2	3
4	5	6	7	8	9	10
11	12	13	14	15	16	17
18	19	20	21	22	23	24
25	26	27	28	29	30	

November 2016

S	M	T	W	T	F	S
		1	2	3	4	5
6	7	8	9	10	11	12
13	14	15	16	17	18	19
20	21	22	23	24	25	26
27	28	29	30			

2016 October

MONDAY
3

TUESDAY
4

WEDNESDAY
5

THURSDAY
6

FRIDAY
7

SATURDAY
8

SUNDAY *First Quarter Moon*
9

Menus

Grocery

There are three ways to get something done: do it yourself, employ someone, or forbid your children to do it.

—Monta Crane

To Do

September 2016

S	M	T	W	T	F	S
				1	2	3
4	5	6	7	8	9	10
11	12	13	14	15	16	17
18	19	20	21	22	23	24
25	26	27	28	29	30	

November 2016

S	M	T	W	T	F	S
		1	2	3	4	5
6	7	8	9	10	11	12
13	14	15	16	17	18	19
20	21	22	23	24	25	26
27	28	29	30			

2016 October

MONDAY *Columbus Day*
Thanksgiving Day (CAN)

10

TUESDAY *Yom Kippur*

11

WEDNESDAY

12

THURSDAY

13

FRIDAY

14

SATURDAY

15

SUNDAY *Sukkot*
Full Moon

16

Menus

Grocery

Like dreams, small creeks grow into mighty rivers.

—Anonymous

To Do

September 2016

S	M	T	W	T	F	S
				1	2	3
4	5	6	7	8	9	10
11	12	13	14	15	16	17
18	19	20	21	22	23	24
25	26	27	28	29	30	

November 2016

S	M	T	W	T	F	S
		1	2	3	4	5
6	7	8	9	10	11	12
13	14	15	16	17	18	19
20	21	22	23	24	25	26
27	28	29	30			

2016 October

MONDAY
17

TUESDAY
18

WEDNESDAY
19

THURSDAY
20

FRIDAY
21

SATURDAY *Last Quarter Moon*
22

SUNDAY
23

Menus

Grocery

Life is like a taxi. The meter just keeps a-ticking whether you are getting somewhere or just standing still.

—Lou Erikson

To Do

September 2016

S	M	T	W	T	F	S
				1	2	3
4	5	6	7	8	9	10
11	12	13	14	15	16	17
18	19	20	21	22	23	24
25	26	27	28	29	30	

November 2016

S	M	T	W	T	F	S
		1	2	3	4	5
6	7	8	9	10	11	12
13	14	15	16	17	18	19
20	21	22	23	24	25	26
27	28	29	30			

2016 October

MONDAY
24

TUESDAY
25

WEDNESDAY
26

THURSDAY
27

FRIDAY
28

SATURDAY
29

SUNDAY *New Moon*
30

Menus

November

SUNDAY	MONDAY	TUESDAY	WEDNESDAY
		1	2
6 *Daylight Saving Time ends*	7	8 *Election Day*	9
13	14	15	16
20	21	22	23
27	28	29	30

2016

THURSDAY	FRIDAY	SATURDAY
3	4	5
10	11 *Veterans Day Remembrance Day (CAN)*	12
17	18	19
24 *Thanksgiving Day*	25	26
	October 2016	December 2016

October 2016

S	M	T	W	T	F	S
						1
2	3	4	5	6	7	8
9	10	11	12	13	14	15
16	17	18	19	20	21	22
23	24	25	26	27	28	29
30	31					

December 2016

S	M	T	W	T	F	S
				1	2	3
4	5	6	7	8	9	10
11	12	13	14	15	16	17
18	19	20	21	22	23	24
25	26	27	28	29	30	31

Monthly Projects

Grocery

The only rock I know that stays steady, the only institution I know that works, is the family.

—Lee Iacocca

To Do

October 2016

S	M	T	W	T	F	S
						1
2	3	4	5	6	7	8
9	10	11	12	13	14	15
16	17	18	19	20	21	22
23	24	25	26	27	28	29
30	31					

December 2016

S	M	T	W	T	F	S
				1	2	3
4	5	6	7	8	9	10
11	12	13	14	15	16	17
18	19	20	21	22	23	24
25	26	27	28	29	30	31

2016 October/November

MONDAY *Halloween*

31

TUESDAY

1

WEDNESDAY

2

THURSDAY

3

FRIDAY

4

SATURDAY

5

SUNDAY *Daylight Saving Time ends*

6

Menus

Grocery

We must teach our children to dream with their eyes open.

—Harry Edwards

To Do

October 2016

S	M	T	W	T	F	S
						1
2	3	4	5	6	7	8
9	10	11	12	13	14	15
16	17	18	19	20	21	22
23	24	25	26	27	28	29
30	31					

December 2016

S	M	T	W	T	F	S
				1	2	3
4	5	6	7	8	9	10
11	12	13	14	15	16	17
18	19	20	21	22	23	24
25	26	27	28	29	30	31

2016 November

MONDAY *First Quarter Moon*

7

TUESDAY *Election Day*

8

WEDNESDAY

9

THURSDAY

10

FRIDAY *Veterans Day*
Remembrance Day (CAN)

11

SATURDAY

12

SUNDAY

13

Menus

Grocery

Our attitude in life determines life's attitude toward us.

—Earl Nightingale

To Do

October 2016

S	M	T	W	T	F	S
						1
2	3	4	5	6	7	8
9	10	11	12	13	14	15
16	17	18	19	20	21	22
23	24	25	26	27	28	29
30	31					

December 2016

S	M	T	W	T	F	S
				1	2	3
4	5	6	7	8	9	10
11	12	13	14	15	16	17
18	19	20	21	22	23	24
25	26	27	28	29	30	31

2016 November

MONDAY *Full Moon*

14

TUESDAY

15

WEDNESDAY

16

THURSDAY

17

FRIDAY

18

SATURDAY

19

SUNDAY

20

Menus

Grocery

Instinct is the nose of the mind.
—Madame de Girardin

To Do

October 2016

S	M	T	W	T	F	S
						1
2	3	4	5	6	7	8
9	10	11	12	13	14	15
16	17	18	19	20	21	22
23	24	25	26	27	28	29
30	31					

December 2016

S	M	T	W	T	F	S
				1	2	3
4	5	6	7	8	9	10
11	12	13	14	15	16	17
18	19	20	21	22	23	24
25	26	27	28	29	30	31

2016 November

MONDAY *Last Quarter Moon*

21

TUESDAY

22

WEDNESDAY

23

THURSDAY *Thanksgiving Day*

24

FRIDAY

25

SATURDAY

26

SUNDAY

27

Menus

December

SUNDAY	MONDAY	TUESDAY	WEDNESDAY
November 2016 S M T W T F S 1 2 3 4 5 6 7 8 9 10 11 12 13 14 15 16 17 18 19 20 21 22 23 24 25 26 27 28 29 30	January 2017 S M T W T F S 1 2 3 4 5 6 7 8 9 10 11 12 13 14 15 16 17 18 19 20 21 22 23 24 25 26 27 28 29 30 31		
4	5	6	7
11	12	13	14
18	19	20	21 *Winter begins*
25 *Christmas Day*	26 *Boxing Day (CAN)* *Kwanzaa*	27	28

2016

THURSDAY	FRIDAY	SATURDAY
1	2	3
8	9	10
15	16	17
22	23	24 *Christmas Eve* *Hanukkah*
29	30	31 *New Year's Eve*

Monthly Projects

Grocery

Real integrity is doing the right thing, knowing that nobody's going to know whether you did it or not.

—Oprah Winfrey

To Do

November 2016

S	M	T	W	T	F	S
		1	2	3	4	5
6	7	8	9	10	11	12
13	14	15	16	17	18	19
20	21	22	23	24	25	26
27	28	29	30			

January 2017

S	M	T	W	T	F	S
1	2	3	4	5	6	7
8	9	10	11	12	13	14
15	16	17	18	19	20	21
22	23	24	25	26	27	28
29	30	31				

2016 November/December

MONDAY
28

TUESDAY *New Moon*
29

WEDNESDAY
30

THURSDAY
1

FRIDAY
2

SATURDAY
3

SUNDAY
4

Menus

Grocery

Service is the rent we pay for the privilege of living on this earth.

—Shirley Chisholm

To Do

November 2016

S	M	T	W	T	F	S
		1	2	3	4	5
6	7	8	9	10	11	12
13	14	15	16	17	18	19
20	21	22	23	24	25	26
27	28	29	30			

January 2017

S	M	T	W	T	F	S
1	2	3	4	5	6	7
8	9	10	11	12	13	14
15	16	17	18	19	20	21
22	23	24	25	26	27	28
29	30	31				

2016 December

MONDAY

5

TUESDAY

6

WEDNESDAY

First Quarter Moon

7

THURSDAY

8

FRIDAY

9

SATURDAY

10

SUNDAY

11

Menus

Grocery

Show me a man who cannot bother to do little things, and I'll show you a man who cannot be trusted to do big things.

—Lawrence D. Bell

To Do

November 2016

S	M	T	W	T	F	S
		1	2	3	4	5
6	7	8	9	10	11	12
13	14	15	16	17	18	19
20	21	22	23	24	25	26
27	28	29	30			

January 2017

S	M	T	W	T	F	S
1	2	3	4	5	6	7
8	9	10	11	12	13	14
15	16	17	18	19	20	21
22	23	24	25	26	27	28
29	30	31				

2016 December

MONDAY
12

TUESDAY
13

WEDNESDAY
14

Full Moon

THURSDAY
15

FRIDAY
16

SATURDAY
17

SUNDAY
18

Menus

Grocery

A baby is born with a need to be loved and never outgrows it.

—Frank A. Clark

To Do

November 2016

S	M	T	W	T	F	S
		1	2	3	4	5
6	7	8	9	10	11	12
13	14	15	16	17	18	19
20	21	22	23	24	25	26
27	28	29	30			

January 2017

S	M	T	W	T	F	S
1	2	3	4	5	6	7
8	9	10	11	12	13	14
15	16	17	18	19	20	21
22	23	24	25	26	27	28
29	30	31				

2016 December

MONDAY
19

TUESDAY
20

WEDNESDAY
21
Winter begins
Last Quarter Moon

THURSDAY
22

FRIDAY
23

SATURDAY
24
Christmas Eve
Hanukkah

SUNDAY
25
Christmas Day

Menus

Grocery

Children are apt to live up to what you believe of them.

—Lady Bird Johnson

To Do

November 2016

S	M	T	W	T	F	S
		1	2	3	4	5
6	7	8	9	10	11	12
13	14	15	16	17	18	19
20	21	22	23	24	25	26
27	28	29	30			

January 2017

S	M	T	W	T	F	S
1	2	3	4	5	6	7
8	9	10	11	12	13	14
15	16	17	18	19	20	21
22	23	24	25	26	27	28
29	30	31				

2016/
2017

December/January

MONDAY *Boxing Day (CAN)*
Kwanzaa

26

TUESDAY

27

WEDNESDAY

28

THURSDAY *New Moon*

29

FRIDAY

30

SATURDAY *New Year's Eve*

31

SUNDAY *New Year's Day*

1

Menus

2017
planning calendar

JANUARY

S	M	T	W	T	F	S
1	2	3	4	5	6	7
8	9	10	11	12	13	14
15	16	17	18	19	20	21
22	23	24	25	26	27	28
29	30	31				

FEBRUARY

S	M	T	W	T	F	S
			1	2	3	4
5	6	7	8	9	10	11
12	13	14	15	16	17	18
19	20	21	22	23	24	25
26	27	28				

MARCH

S	M	T	W	T	F	S
			1	2	3	4
5	6	7	8	9	10	11
12	13	14	15	16	17	18
19	20	21	22	23	24	25
26	27	28	29	30	31	

APRIL

S	M	T	W	T	F	S
						1
2	3	4	5	6	7	8
9	10	11	12	13	14	15
16	17	18	19	20	21	22
23/30	24	25	26	27	28	29

MAY

S	M	T	W	T	F	S
	1	2	3	4	5	6
7	8	9	10	11	12	13
14	15	16	17	18	19	20
21	22	23	24	25	26	27
28	29	30	31			

JUNE

S	M	T	W	T	F	S
				1	2	3
4	5	6	7	8	9	10
11	12	13	14	15	16	17
18	19	20	21	22	23	24
25	26	27	28	29	30	

2017
planning calendar

JULY

S	M	T	W	T	F	S
						1
2	3	4	5	6	7	8
9	10	11	12	13	14	15
16	17	18	19	20	21	22
23/30	24/31	25	26	27	28	29

AUGUST

S	M	T	W	T	F	S
		1	2	3	4	5
6	7	8	9	10	11	12
13	14	15	16	17	18	19
20	21	22	23	24	25	26
27	28	29	30	31		

SEPTEMBER

S	M	T	W	T	F	S
					1	2
3	4	5	6	7	8	9
10	11	12	13	14	15	16
17	18	19	20	21	22	23
24	25	26	27	28	29	30

OCTOBER

S	M	T	W	T	F	S
1	2	3	4	5	6	7
8	9	10	11	12	13	14
15	16	17	18	19	20	21
22	23	24	25	26	27	28
29	30	31				

NOVEMBER

S	M	T	W	T	F	S
			1	2	3	4
5	6	7	8	9	10	11
12	13	14	15	16	17	18
19	20	21	22	23	24	25
26	27	28	29	30		

DECEMBER

S	M	T	W	T	F	S
					1	2
3	4	5	6	7	8	9
10	11	12	13	14	15	16
17	18	19	20	21	22	23
24/31	25	26	27	28	29	30

Notes

Notes

Notes

Notes

Notes

Notes

Notes

Babysitter Information

You are at:

Name: ______________________________

Address: ______________________________

City: ______________ State: __________ Zip: __________

The phone number here is:

____

In case of an emergency, call 911

and: ______________________________

Poison Control: ______________________________

Our Cell/Pager # is:

____

We will be at:

Meal/Snack Instructions...

Place self-stick note pad here.

Let Us Introduce Our Children

Name: ______________________________

Age: ______________ Bedtime: ______________

Likes/Dislikes: ______________________________

Favorite Things: ______________________________

Allergies/Medical: ______________________________

Name: ______________________________

Age: ______________ Bedtime: ______________

Likes/Dislikes: ______________________________

Favorite Things: ______________________________

Allergies/Medical: ______________________________

Name: ______________________________

Age: ______________ Bedtime: ______________

Likes/Dislikes: ______________________________

Favorite Things: ______________________________

Allergies/Medical: ______________________________

Name: ______________________________

Age: ______________ Bedtime: ______________

Likes/Dislikes: ______________________________

Favorite Things: ______________________________

Allergies/Medical: ______________________________

Babysitters' Phone Numbers

Name:	Phone Number:

Children's Play Friends

Name:	Parent:	Phone Number:

Quick Reference Children's Organizations

Child's Name: ______________________
Organization/Team: ______________________

____

Leader: ______________________
Phone: ______________________
Meeting/Practice:
M__ T__ W__ TH__ F__ S__ SU__
Carpool: ______________________
Snacks/Refreshments: ______________________

____

____

Child's Name: ______________________
Organization/Team: ______________________

____

Leader: ______________________
Phone: ______________________
Meeting/Practice:
M__ T__ W__ TH__ F__ S__ SU__
Carpool: ______________________
Snacks/Refreshments: ______________________

____

____

Child's Name: ______________________
Organization/Team: ______________________

____

Leader: ______________________
Phone: ______________________
Meeting/Practice:
M__ T__ W__ TH__ F__ S__ SU__
Carpool: ______________________
Snacks/Refreshments: ______________________

____

____

Child's Name: ______________________
Organization/Team: ______________________

____

Leader: ______________________
Phone: ______________________
Meeting/Practice:
M__ T__ W__ TH__ F__ S__ SU__
Carpool: ______________________
Snacks/Refreshments: ______________________

____

____

Child's Name: ______________________
Organization/Team: ______________________

____

Leader: ______________________
Phone: ______________________
Meeting/Practice:
M__ T__ W__ TH__ F__ S__ SU__
Carpool: ______________________
Snacks/Refreshments: ______________________

____

____

Child's Name: ______________________
Organization/Team: ______________________

____

Leader: ______________________
Phone: ______________________
Meeting/Practice:
M__ T__ W__ TH__ F__ S__ SU__
Carpool: ______________________
Snacks/Refreshments: ______________________

____

____

Quick Reference Parents' Organizations

Child's Name: ____________________
Organization/Team: ________________

Leader: ____________________
Phone: ____________________
Meeting/Practice:
M__ T__ W__ TH__ F__ S__ SU__
Carpool: ____________________
Snacks/Refreshments: ____________

Child's Name: ____________________
Organization/Team: ________________

Leader: ____________________
Phone: ____________________
Meeting/Practice:
M__ T__ W__ TH__ F__ S__ SU__
Carpool: ____________________
Snacks/Refreshments: ____________

Child's Name: ____________________
Organization/Team: ________________

Leader: ____________________
Phone: ____________________
Meeting/Practice:
M__ T__ W__ TH__ F__ S__ SU__
Carpool: ____________________
Snacks/Refreshments: ____________

Child's Name: ____________________
Organization/Team: ________________

Leader: ____________________
Phone: ____________________
Meeting/Practice:
M__ T__ W__ TH__ F__ S__ SU__
Carpool: ____________________
Snacks/Refreshments: ____________

Child's Name: ____________________
Organization/Team: ________________

Leader: ____________________
Phone: ____________________
Meeting/Practice:
M__ T__ W__ TH__ F__ S__ SU__
Carpool: ____________________
Snacks/Refreshments: ____________

Child's Name: ____________________
Organization/Team: ________________

Leader: ____________________
Phone: ____________________
Meeting/Practice:
M__ T__ W__ TH__ F__ S__ SU__
Carpool: ____________________
Snacks/Refreshments: ____________

Quick Reference Address/Phone

Name:

Address:

City:

State/Zip:

Home Phone:

Work Phone:

Fax: Cell:

Email:

Name:

Address:

City:

State/Zip:

Home Phone:

Work Phone:

Fax: Cell:

Email:

Name:

Address:

City:

State/Zip:

Home Phone:

Work Phone:

Fax: Cell:

Email:

Name:

Address:

City:

State/Zip:

Home Phone:

Work Phone:

Fax: Cell:

Email:

Name:

Address:

City:

State/Zip:

Home Phone:

Work Phone:

Fax: Cell:

Email:

Name:

Address:

City:

State/Zip:

Home Phone:

Work Phone:

Fax: Cell:

Email:

Quick Reference Address/Phone

Name: ____________________

Address: ____________________

City: ____________________

State/Zip: ____________________

Home Phone: ____________________

Work Phone: ____________________

Fax: __________ Cell: __________

Email: ____________________

Name: ____________________

Address: ____________________

City: ____________________

State/Zip: ____________________

Home Phone: ____________________

Work Phone: ____________________

Fax: __________ Cell: __________

Email: ____________________

Name: ____________________

Address: ____________________

City: ____________________

State/Zip: ____________________

Home Phone: ____________________

Work Phone: ____________________

Fax: __________ Cell: __________

Email: ____________________

Name: ____________________

Address: ____________________

City: ____________________

State/Zip: ____________________

Home Phone: ____________________

Work Phone: ____________________

Fax: __________ Cell: __________

Email: ____________________

Name: ____________________

Address: ____________________

City: ____________________

State/Zip: ____________________

Home Phone: ____________________

Work Phone: ____________________

Fax: __________ Cell: __________

Email: ____________________

Name: ____________________

Address: ____________________

City: ____________________

State/Zip: ____________________

Home Phone: ____________________

Work Phone: ____________________

Fax: __________ Cell: __________

Email: ____________________

Quick Reference Address/Phone

Name: ______________________
Address: ______________________
City: ______________________
State/Zip: ______________________
Home Phone: ______________________
Work Phone: ______________________
Fax: __________ Cell: __________
Email: ______________________

Name: ______________________
Address: ______________________
City: ______________________
State/Zip: ______________________
Home Phone: ______________________
Work Phone: ______________________
Fax: __________ Cell: __________
Email: ______________________

Name: ______________________
Address: ______________________
City: ______________________
State/Zip: ______________________
Home Phone: ______________________
Work Phone: ______________________
Fax: __________ Cell: __________
Email: ______________________

Name: ______________________
Address: ______________________
City: ______________________
State/Zip: ______________________
Home Phone: ______________________
Work Phone: ______________________
Fax: __________ Cell: __________
Email: ______________________

Name: ______________________
Address: ______________________
City: ______________________
State/Zip: ______________________
Home Phone: ______________________
Work Phone: ______________________
Fax: __________ Cell: __________
Email: ______________________

Name: ______________________
Address: ______________________
City: ______________________
State/Zip: ______________________
Home Phone: ______________________
Work Phone: ______________________
Fax: __________ Cell: __________
Email: ______________________

Quick Reference Web Address/Login

Web Address/URL: ______________________________

Login Name: ______________ Date Assigned: ______________

Password: ______________ Renewal Date: ______________

Web Address/URL: ______________________________

Login Name: ______________ Date Assigned: ______________

Password: ______________ Renewal Date: ______________

Web Address/URL: ______________________________

Login Name: ______________ Date Assigned: ______________

Password: ______________ Renewal Date: ______________

Web Address/URL: ______________________________

Login Name: ______________ Date Assigned: ______________

Password: ______________ Renewal Date: ______________

Web Address/URL: ______________________________

Login Name: ______________ Date Assigned: ______________

Password: ______________ Renewal Date: ______________

Quick Reference Web Address/Login

Web Address/URL: ____________________

Login Name: ____________ Date Assigned: ____________

Password: ____________ Renewal Date: ____________

Web Address/URL: ____________________

Login Name: ____________ Date Assigned: ____________

Password: ____________ Renewal Date: ____________

Web Address/URL: ____________________

Login Name: ____________ Date Assigned: ____________

Password: ____________ Renewal Date: ____________

Web Address/URL: ____________________

Login Name: ____________ Date Assigned: ____________

Password: ____________ Renewal Date: ____________

Web Address/URL: ____________________

Login Name: ____________ Date Assigned: ____________

Password: ____________ Renewal Date: ____________

Additional Phone Numbers

Church: ____________________

Hair Salon: ____________________

Library: ____________________

Attorney: ____________________

Accountant: ____________________

Bank: ____________________

Bank: ____________________

Insurance Agency: ____________________

Post Office: ____________________

Veterinarian: ____________________

Favorite Restaurants:

____

____

____

Travel Agent: ____________________

Florist: ____________________

Other Numbers:

Name:	Number:

Notes